GHOST SHIPS

BY LISA OWINGS

EPIC

BELLWETHER MEDIA • MINNEAPOLIS, MN

EPIC

EPIC BOOKS are no ordinary books. They burst with intense action, high-speed heroics, and shadows of the unknown. Are you ready for an Epic adventure?

This edition first published in 2015 by Bellwether Media, Inc.

No part of this publication may be reproduced in whole or in part without written permission of the publisher. For information regarding permission, write to Bellwether Media, Inc., Attention: Permissions Department, 5357 Penn Avenue South, Minneapolis, MN 55419.

Library of Congress Cataloging-in-Publication Data

Owings, Lisa, author.
  Ghost Ships / by Lisa Owings.
    pages cm. – (Epic. Unexplained Mysteries)
  Includes bibliographical references and index.
  Summary: "Engaging images accompany information about ghost ships. The combination of high-interest subject matter and light text is intended for students in grades 2 through 7"– Provided by publisher.
  Audience: Ages 7-12.
  ISBN 978-1-62617-202-9 (hardcover : alk. paper)
  1. Curiosities and wonders–Juvenile literature. 2. Apparitions–Juvenile literature. 3. Shipwrecks–Juvenile literature. I. Title.
  AG195.O95 2015
  001.94–dc23
                    2014036513

Designed by Jon Eppard.

Printed in the United States of America, North Mankato, MN.

TABLE OF CONTENTS

AHOY! ANYONE ABOARD?

A ship sails toward harbor. The full moon shines in the night sky. By its light, the captain sees another ship in the distance. But its sails are torn. And no one is on deck.

The captain pulls up beside the strange ship. His crew searches it. Its tables are set and all is in order. But not a soul is found aboard. Could the ship be haunted?

HAUNTED SEAS

A ghost ship is a boat that sails with no one aboard. For centuries, sailors have told of **deserted** ships that haunt the seas.

Some ghost ships are real. They are found drifting and empty. There may be no signs of trouble. It looks like the crew simply disappeared.

WITHOUT A CREW

The *Mary Celeste* was found drifting in the Atlantic Ocean in 1872. It was in perfect order. But its captain and crew were missing. No one can explain what happened.

Mary Celeste

FOREVER AT SEA

Many old tales tell of the Flying Dutchman. The ship was cursed, and all its crew members died. But their spirits are doomed to sail forever.

Other ghost ships may not be real. Stories tell of **cursed** ships with ghostly crews. Sailors claim **visions** of ships that sank long ago.

NORMAL OR PARANORMAL?

Some people believe ghost ships are truly haunted. Travelers report seeing **vanishing** ships or **skeleton** crews. They think some ships are sailed by spirits.

16

Deserted ships are **eerie**. People often turn to the **paranormal** for explanation. They think sea monsters, angry ghosts, or **aliens** might be to blame.

FROZEN IN TIME

Stories say the *Octavius* was found in 1775. Everyone on the ship was frozen. The last log entry was written in 1762. The icy crew may have sailed the Arctic for 13 years.

Skeptics find normal reasons for deserted ships. Their crews might have fallen overboard. Perhaps they left the ship in panic. Some could have even been taken by pirates.

The Bermuda Triangle

THE BERMUDA TRIANGLE

The *Carroll A. Deering* was found without a crew in 1921. It had just sailed through the Bermuda Triangle. Searches for the crew came up empty.

FAMOUS GHOST SHIPS

GHOST SHIP OF NORTHUMBERLAND STRAIT:
1700s to Present
Visions of a burning ship are often seen in Canadian waters.

SEA BIRD: 1850
This ship was found off the U.S. coast. Water was boiling on the stove. But only a dog and cat were aboard.

SS VALENCIA: 1906
A lifeboat from this ship turned up in Canadian waters. People claim to have seen skeletons rowing it.

SS OURANG MEDAN: 1947
This ship is said to have been found near Indonesia. Its whole crew was dead. The ship caught on fire before anyone could find out what happened.

KAZ II: 2007
This boat was drifting near Australia. The engine was running and food was laid out. But there was no trace of the crew.

Even today, ghost ships still roam the seas. Are their crews just unlucky? Or do strange and dark things truly **lurk** among the waves?

GLOSSARY

aliens—beings from another planet

cursed—under an evil spell

deserted—empty

eerie—creepy

lurk—to hide while waiting to do something bad

paranormal—not able to be explained by science

skeleton—a set of bones

skeptics—people who doubt the truth of something

vanishing—disappearing suddenly

visions—things seen that could be real or imagined

TO LEARN MORE

At the Library

Hawkins, John. *The World's Strangest Unexplained Mysteries.* New York, N.Y.: PowerKids Press, 2012.

Higgins, Nadia. *Ghosts.* Minneapolis, Minn.: Bellwether Media, 2014.

McClellan, Ray. *The Bermuda Triangle.* Minneapolis, Minn.: Bellwether Media, 2014.

On the Web

Learning more about ghost ships is as easy as 1, 2, 3.

1. Go to www.factsurfer.com.

2. Enter "ghost ships" into the search box.

3. Click the "Surf" button and you will see a list of related web sites.

With factsurfer.com, finding more information is just a click away.

INDEX

The images in this book are reproduced through the courtesy of: Jon Eppard, front cover, pp. 6-7, 8-9, 10, 12-13, 14, 16-17, 19 (top, bottom); Melkor3D, pp. 4-5; De Agostini Picture Library/ AgeFotostock, p. 11; LindaMarieB, p. 15; Mary Evans Picture Library/ Alamy, p. 18; Algol, p. 21.